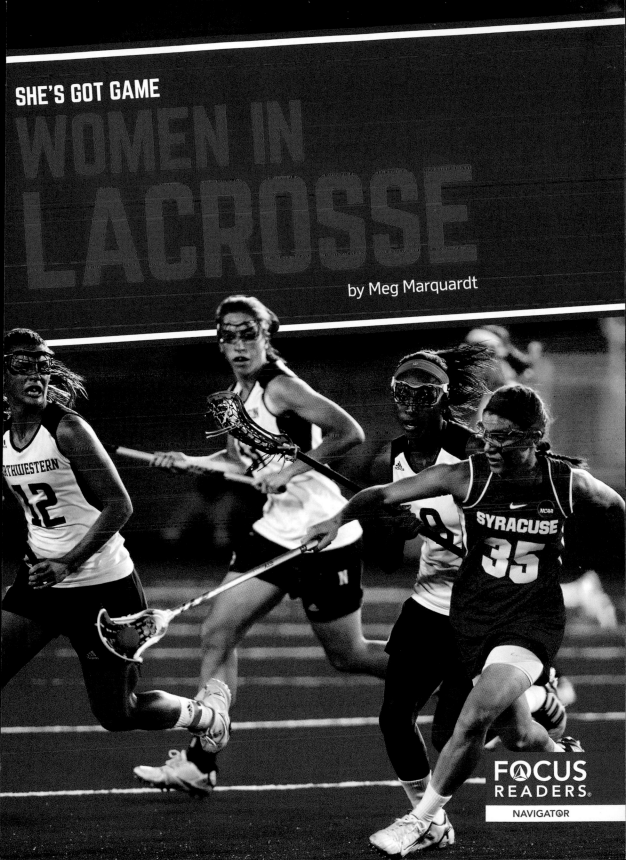

SHE'S GOT GAME

WOMEN IN LACROSSE

by Meg Marquardt

FOCUS
READERS.

NAVIGATOR

WWW.FOCUSREADERS.COM

Focus Readers is distributed by North Star Editions:
sales@northstareditions.com | 888-417-0195

Produced for Focus Readers by Red Line Editorial.

Photographs ©: John Dunn/AP Images, cover, 1; Jan Karwowski/EPA/Rex Features, 4–5; Daniel Kucin Jr./Icon Sportswire, 7, 23; Matthias Hangst/Bongarts/Getty Images, 9; duncan1890/iStockphoto, 10–11; Bettmann/Getty Images, 13; Hulton Deutsch/Corbis Historical/Getty Images, 15; Professional Sport/Popperfoto/Getty Images, 16–17; Katsumi Kasahara/AP Images, 19; Carlos Gonzalez/Minneapolis Star Tribune/Zumapress.com/Newscom, 21; Aspen Photo/Shutterstock Images, 24–25; Tony Quinn/Icon Sportswire, 27; Richard T Gagnon/Getty Images Sport/Getty Images, 29

Library of Congress Cataloging-in-Publication Data
Names: Marquardt, Meg, author.
Title: Women in lacrosse / by Meg Marquardt.
Description: Lake Elmo, MN : Focus Readers, [2020] | Series: She's got game |
    Includes index. | Audience: Grades 4-6
Identifiers: LCCN 2019036061 (print) | LCCN 2019036062 (ebook) | ISBN
    9781644930618 (hardcover) | ISBN 9781644931400 (paperback) | ISBN
    9781644932988 (pdf) | ISBN 9781644932193 (ebook)
Subjects: LCSH: Lacrosse for women--History--Juvenile literature. |
    Lacrosse players--Biography--Juvenile literature.
Classification: LCC GV989.15 .M37 2020 (print) | LCC GV989.15 (ebook) |
    DDC 796.36/2082--dc23
LC record available at https://lccn.loc.gov/2019036061
LC ebook record available at https://lccn.loc.gov/2019036062

Printed in the United States of America
Mankato, MN
012020

ABOUT THE AUTHOR

Meg Marquardt has been playing sports since she was a little girl. Today, she loves to research and write about all types of games and sports. She lives in Madison, Wisconsin, with her two scientist cats, Lagrange and Doppler.

TABLE OF CONTENTS

CHAPTER 1

GOING FOR GOLD

On July 30, 2017, two lacrosse teams faced off in Wroclaw, Poland. Canada and the United States were playing in the finals of the World Games. The US women's national team had not lost a game in the tournament. Canada and the United States were tied 6–6. Nearly 30 minutes of play remained.

To reach the 2017 World Games finals, Team USA defeated many teams, including Poland.

The US players took control. They scored five straight goals. Brooke Griffin scored two of those goals. The US team also stopped Canada from scoring for more than 24 minutes. But with less than six minutes left, the Canadian team mounted a comeback. Players scored two quick goals. The score was 11–8. In lacrosse, three goals can be scored in almost no time at all.

Canadian player Kaylin Morissette cradled the ball. She and her team drove down the field. But the US defenders and goalie were ready. They cornered Morissette. With quick stickwork, they forced a turnover. A US player scooped up

Brooke Griffin (right) was a star midfielder at the University of Maryland.

the ball. The US team kept the ball away from the Canadian team. The clock ran out. The United States had won the World Games!

The World Games is an event for sports that are not in the Olympics. But playing in the World Games can help a sport get added to the Olympics. The 2017 Games was the first year that lacrosse was part of the event. Lacrosse did not have a full competition. It appeared as an invitational sport. The event was like a tryout for the sport. Only six women's teams played. They needed to perform well and bring out big crowds. If the tryout went well, lacrosse could be an **officially sanctioned** sport during the next World Games.

Those six women's teams played hard. They made a great impression. The World

British players challenge Japan's Sachiko Komine during the 2017 World Games.

Games invited women's lacrosse back for a full tournament in 2021. The World Games also invited men's lacrosse as an invitational sport. As people work to bring lacrosse to the Olympics, female athletes are leading the way.

CHAPTER 2

EARLY YEARS

Lacrosse has been played for hundreds of years. The first lacrosse players were **indigenous** peoples of North America. Many nations played lacrosse, including Cherokee and Onondaga peoples. European settlers first saw the sport in the 1630s. Settlers in Canada began playing lacrosse in the 1800s.

A drawing shows a lacrosse match between Canadian and Iroquois players in the late 1800s.

In 1884, Louisa Lumsden watched a lacrosse game in Montreal, Quebec. Lumsden was the head of St. Leonards, a school in Scotland. When she returned home, she brought lacrosse to her school. Girls at the school played their first game in 1890. That game marked the beginning of modern women's lacrosse.

INDIGENOUS LACROSSE

Indigenous nations played different versions of lacrosse. For example, Cherokee people played with one stick in each hand. Winnebago people used one stick per player. But the stick had a small net. It was barely bigger than the ball. In contrast, Iroquoian sticks had large nets. These sticks became the basis for modern lacrosse sticks.

Bryn Mawr's lacrosse team poses for a picture in the 1920s.

A St. Leonards's graduate brought the game back to the United States. Rosabelle Sinclair led the athletics department at Bryn Mawr School in Maryland. She convinced parents that the game was safe. In 1926, Sinclair formed the first US women's lacrosse school team.

Women's lacrosse is similar to men's lacrosse in many ways. But one difference sets the two games apart. In men's lacrosse, players can make full physical contact with one another. In women's lacrosse, player contact is more limited.

In the 1930s, women's lacrosse spread across the northeastern United States. The sport also grew in the United Kingdom and Australia. However, its growth slowed for several decades.

Many people thought women's lacrosse was as rough as men's lacrosse. Some also believed women should not play rough sports. In response, Sinclair and others focused on the game's

British and US players compete for the ball during a match in the 1950s.

gracefulness. They appealed to the public's ideas about female **gender roles**.

Many players wanted lacrosse to remain an **amateur** sport. They did not want the sport to have pro leagues, as baseball did. As a result, lacrosse had less opportunity to spread.

CHAPTER 3

NEW GROWTH

In the 1970s, women's lacrosse began growing quickly. More schools across the United States added women's teams. In 1982, the National Collegiate Athletic Association (NCAA) held its first national championship for the sport. That same year, six national teams played in the first Women's Lacrosse World Cup.

Lois Richardson was one of the United Kingdom's star players in the 1982 World Cup.

17

The United States faced Australia in the final game. At halftime, Australia was up 6–1. But the US team had a plan. Anne Brooking started guarding the top Australian scorer. Brooking followed her on the field wherever she went. The United States stormed back to tie

NEW STICKS

For much of the 1900s, most lacrosse sticks were made by hand. Mohawk people produced more than 90 percent of all lacrosse sticks. These sticks were built from wood. In 1970, a company produced the first lacrosse sticks with plastic heads. Machines could make a lot of these sticks at one time. The sticks were also cheaper than handmade sticks. These new sticks helped the sport of lacrosse grow.

An English defender challenges a Scottish player during the 1997 World Cup.

the game. In overtime, they defeated Australia 10–7.

The 1982 World Cup was just the beginning for many lacrosse stars. Sue Sofarnos was one of those players. She helped Australia win gold four years later. In 1997, Sofarnos played in her fifth straight World Cup. Vivien Jones also played in her fifth World Cup that year. She was one of Wales's best players.

In 2001, Jones played in her sixth World Cup. During her career, she played a record 108 **international** games.

In 2009, the Haudenosaunee national team played in its first Women's World Cup. This team represents the six indigenous nations of the Iroquois Confederacy. Their nations' peoples were among the world's first lacrosse players.

The popularity of lacrosse has exploded since the early 2000s. Before that, the sport was mostly limited to the northeastern United States. But by 2019, high schools in 35 states fielded girls' lacrosse teams. The sport's future looked brighter than ever.

Minnesota high school players compete for the ball during a 2012 game.

TAYLOR CUMMINGS

Taylor Cummings was born in Virginia in 1994. She played lacrosse at McDonogh School. This high school was known for its girls' lacrosse team. Taylor played midfielder. For three straight years, the team did not lose a game. Taylor also led the team to four state championships.

In 2013, Taylor Cummings started playing for the University of Maryland. In her first year, she scored 43 goals. She was also incredible at controlling **draws**. The next year, she won the Tewaaraton Award. That award is given to the best women's college lacrosse player. Cummings was the youngest person to win that award. In 2016, she became the first player, male or female, to win the award three times.

In 2017, Cummings led Team USA to two gold medals. The team first won the Women's

Taylor Cummings runs with the ball during a 2016 game.

World Cup. Then it won the World Games. In 2018, Cummings began playing professionally. She joined the New York Fight. Many fans agreed she was leading the sport of women's lacrosse.

CHAPTER 4

LOOKING AHEAD

During the 2010s, lacrosse was one of the fastest-growing US sports. The first two women's professional leagues started during that time. College women's lacrosse grew as well. Between 2006 and 2016, the number of college players in the sport nearly doubled. This growth was not only about numbers, however.

A Temple player passes the ball during a 2012 game against Delaware.

For many decades, lacrosse players have been mostly white. In 2016, college women's lacrosse players were still 86 percent white. However, the number of nonwhite players had nearly tripled since 2008.

HARLEM LACROSSE

Schools in East Harlem, New York, have had high dropout rates for many years. In 2008, a group of people wanted to help more students graduate. They recruited middle school students to play lacrosse. The group succeeded. By 2019, their work had spread to five cities. Hundreds of girls were playing lacrosse because of their group. Almost all of them were nonwhite. These students' graduation rates were higher than that of their peers.

A Hofstra player clashes with a Johns Hopkins player during a 2018 NCAA game.

In addition, more of the sport's stars have been nonwhite. For example, Joey Coffey played midfield and defense for Cornell University. As a black woman, she faced racism on and off the field.

But she remained focused on her game. She excelled at controlling draws. In 2016, she was an All-American.

Technology has also helped more women play lacrosse. In 2016, college player Noelle Lambert got in a car accident. Her left leg was amputated, or cut off, at the knee. Doctors made her a running blade. This is a type of **prosthetic** leg for athletes. In 2018, Lambert rejoined her college team. She scored a goal her first game back.

In 2017, more than 300,000 women and girls in the United States played lacrosse. Stars such as Lambert and Coffey have helped bring new players

Noelle Lambert warms up before a 2018 NCAA game.

to the sport. Fans can expect more new talent to continue to push women's lacrosse to new heights.

FOCUS ON
WOMEN IN LACROSSE

Write your answers on a separate piece of paper.

1. Write a paragraph that describes Iroquois peoples' relationship to lacrosse.

2. Do you think women's lacrosse should allow physical contact? Why or why not?

3. In 1982, which team won the first Women's Lacrosse World Cup?

> **A.** United States
> **B.** Australia
> **C.** Wales

4. Why might machine-made lacrosse sticks have helped the sport grow?

> **A.** The new sticks lasted longer.
> **B.** The new sticks were more beautiful.
> **C.** The new sticks were more affordable.

Answer key on page 32.

GLOSSARY

amateur
Having to do with an activity played for enjoyment rather than money.

draws
Events in which one player from each lacrosse team competes for control of the ball, occurring after goals and at the start of halves.

gender roles
Social behaviors that a culture expects of certain genders.

indigenous
Native to a region, or belonging to ancestors who did not immigrate to the region.

international
Having to do with many different countries.

officially sanctioned
Able to compete for medals.

prosthetic
Having to do with artificial body parts.

TO LEARN MORE

BOOKS

Kortemeier, Todd. *Greatest Moments in Women's Sports.*
  Minneapolis: Abdo Publishing, 2018.
Myers, Jess. *Make Me the Best Lacrosse Player.*
  Minneapolis: Abdo Publishing, 2017.
Williams, Heather. *Girls' Lacrosse: A Guide for Players and
  Fans.* North Mankato, MN: Capstone Press, 2019.

NOTE TO EDUCATORS

Visit **www.focusreaders.com** to find lesson plans,
activities, links, and other resources related to this title.

INDEX

Answer Key: **1.** Answers will vary; **2.** Answers will vary; **3.** A; **4.** C